1. Introduction

1.1 Preamble

1.2 Modelling vs. Modeling

1.3 Copyright Information

2. Background Information

2.1 The Graphics Library

2.2 The Graphics Modeller

2.3 The Graphics Renderer

3. Installation Instructions

3.1 Warning

3.2 Download the Software

3.3 Install the Graphics Library

3.4 Install the Graphics Renderer

3.5 Install the Graphics Modeller

3.6 Clean Up

4. Miscellaneous Information

4.1 Lighting

4.2 Tutorials

5. Related Links

5.1 Graphics Libraries

5.2 Graphics Renderers

5.3 Graphics Modellers

5.4 Miscellaneous Links

6. Acknowledgements

1. Introduction

1.1. Preamble

This document will guide you through the steps used to install and configure an environment for modelling and rendering three-dimensional graphics using Linux. In this section you will also find information in laymans terms about the required components and how they piece together. The installation section is purposely minimal; merely the quick and dirty steps needed to take to get up and running (if it doesn't work, more information is available). For those that want more information about the software components and what they do (in general), please continue reading.

There are, at the minimum, three software packages you'll need in order to get up and running. These are as follows (in the order they are explained, not the order they are installed):

$\sum$ a graphics library;

$\sum$ a graphics modeller;

Σ a graphics renderer.

1.2. Modelling vs. Modeling

The spelling modelling is Canadian. The spelling modeling is American. The original author of this document is Canadian. ;-)

1.3. Copyright Information

∑ if you distribute this work in part, instructions for obtaining the complete version of this manual must be included, and a means for obtaining a complete version provided;

∑ small portions may be reproduced as illustrations for reviews or quotes in other works without this permission notice if proper citation is given.

2. Background Information

The content of this section exists only to describe, in general, the three main components required for three-dimensional modelling and rendering with a Linux-based system.

2.1. The Graphics Library

A graphics library consists of the most basic tools used for manipulating graphical images. Think of all the things needed to build a house: wiring, plumbing, wood, bricks, and such. The graphics library can be thought of as not these items, but rather the tools used create such items. After all, wire, metal tubes, planks, and bricks don't magically appear; rather they are created and formed as entities unto themselves. On a similar note, graphics don't magically appear on the screen — typically they consist of lower-level graphics primitives (lines, rectangles, and individual pixels, for example).

So the graphics library, then, can be thought of as the low-level graphics primitives used to build more complex objects (spheres, boxes, complex polygons, etc.). Those complex objects are then used to build even more complicated shapes and figures.

The graphics library installed was the freeware implementation of OpenGL called Mesa.

2.2. The Graphics Modeller

Since the graphics renderer is, ideally, completely hidden from the end-user, we'll deal with that last (besides which, modelling is the next logical step in keeping with my house-building analogy). However, when it comes to the actual installation, a graphics modeller relies on the renderer already being installed.

If the graphics library is akin to the tools used to build the tools used to build a house (!), then graphics modellers can be thought of as the tools used to build the blueprints for the house — sophisticated blueprints, as modellers let you dictate exactly where the wiring, plumbing, wood panels, bricks, and forth are supposed to go. Furthermore, they let you pick the style of panelling and the colour of the bricks you desire.

The graphics modeller installed was the freeware package called The
Mops, which produces RenderMan-compatible files.

2.3. The Graphics Renderer

In keeping with the house-building analogy, the graphics renderer is
then the construction workers. Once you have the blueprints and
materials ready to go, you need something to actually build the house
so it appears how it was designed. The graphics renderer is given
information (i.e., the blueprints in the form of a RenderMan-compatible file,
or equivalent) from the the modeller to produce the
final result.

Just as the graphics modeller needs the graphics renderer before it
can be installed, the renderer relies on the graphics library being
installed beforehand.

The graphics renderer installed was the Blue Moon Rendering Toolkit
which uses RenderMan files.

3. Installation Instructions

Keep in mind that these are brief instructions; a quick summary of the
more important details you'll find listed in README files for the
corresponding software packages. It is, by no means, a substitute for
actually reading those files (as they contain copyright information
and other instructions not necessarily covered by this document).

3.1. Warning

First, let it be known that this document only covers how to get up
and running using RedHat v7.0. Whenever given the choice as to which
software package to download, please make sure it is compatible with
the flavour of Linux you happen to be running.

Second, please only send E-mail if you have information that would be
helpful to other people who might read this document (such as
explaining how to install other tools, pointers to other tutorials,
missing steps grammar and/or speling mistakes and/or tpyos, etc.). If
software doesn't compile, or you can't figure it out, please read its
accompanying documentation. Please understand that your system may be

completely different, and as such debugging problems via E-mail across
the Internet is not a task anyone enjoys. ;-)

Third, these are software packages that installed without any severe
hitches (read: severe headaches). In the Related Links section, there
are alternate software packages along side the ones covered below.
Note that just because a given software package is not covered in
depth does not mean it is any worse (or better) than those chosen to
install.

Good luck!

3.2. Download the Software

Before you begin, you will need a web browser and Unix shell. If you
don't know how to use a shell [bash, ksh, etc.], you're own your own
(although instructions are given in both English and shell commands).

Unless otherwise specified, all instructions are to be carried out as
root.

1. Create a new directory *usr*local/archives for the packages:

mkdir *usr*local/archives

2. Download the following packages (in .tar.gz form) into the newly
created directory (homepages are given, as well as links to
download pages, and minimum software version):

∑ Mesa Graphics Library <http://www.mesa3d.org/> v3.4.1:
www.mesa3d.org/download.html <http://www.mesa3d.org/download.html>

∑ Blue Moon Rendering Toolkit <http://www.bmrt.org/> v2.6beta:
www.bmrt.org/BMRTdownload/index.html
<http://www.bmrt.org/BMRTdownload/index.html>

∑ The Mops <http://www.informatik.uni-rostock.de/~rschultz/mops/>
v0.42d: www.informatik.uni-rostock.de/~rschultz/mops/download.html
<http://www.informatik.uni-rostock.de/~rschultz/mops/download.html>

3.3. Install the Graphics Library

Old versions of tar do not support the z argument. For those systems,
leave out the z argument and use gunzip on the file before using tar.

1. Change to the *usr*local/archives directory:

cd *usr*local/archives

2. Extract Mesa (substitute version number where required):

tar zxf MesaLib-3.4.1.tar.gz

tar zxf MesaDemos-3.4.1.tar.gz

3. Change to the MesaLib subdirectory:

cd Mesa-3.4.1

4. Configure, make, and install Mesa with the following sequence of
commands:

./configure; make; make install

5. Edit *etc*ld.so.conf, and ensure you have a line that reads:

*usr*local/lib

6. Run the dynamic library configuration program:

ldconfig

3.4. Install the Graphics Renderer

1. Return to the *usr*local/archives directory:

cd ..

2. Extract the Blue Moon Rendering Toolkit (substitute version number where required):

tar zxf BMRT2.6beta.linux-glibc2.tar.gz

3. Change to the BMRT subdirectory:

cd BMRT2.6

4. Copy files to appropriate destination directories:

cp bin/* *usr*local/bin/

cp lib/lib* *usr*local/lib/

cp include/* *usr*local/include/

5. Make a directory for the shaders, ensure it is world-writable, then copy the shader files into it:

mkdir *usr*local/shaders

chmod 777 *usr*local/shaders

cp shaders/*.sl* *usr*local/shaders/

cp shaders/*.h *usr*local/shaders/

cp examples/*.sl* *usr*local/shaders/

cp examples/*.h *usr*local/shaders/

6. Edit the system login profile (*etc*profile or equivalent), and add the line:

export SHADERS=.:*usr*local/shaders

7. Copy the .rendribrc file to each user's home directory.

If anything goes wrong, please consult the README file that
accompanies the Blue Moon Rendering Toolkit, or visit their website.

3.5. Install the Graphics Modeller

The Mops may be installed on a per-user basis, or on a system-wide
basis by root (or equivalent). In this example, it is installed using
a non-administrative account, which should yield positive results.
Note that the compile failed during the install (missing a C header
file), so the precompiled binaries (compatible with RedHat v6.0, your
system may vary) were installed, as follows:

1. Change to one directory above where you'd like The Mops to reside.
For example, if *usr*local/mops was desired, then issue the
following command:

cd *usr*local

2. Extract the mops (substitute number where required), then change
into its directory:

tar zxf *usr*local/archives/mops-0.42d-BMRT26-linux.tar.gz

cd mops

3. Move the following files from *usr*local/mops/src to
*usr*local/mops:

mv src/crtmopssh.sh .

mv src/mfio.so .

mv src/mops .

4. Copy the .mopsrc file to the home directory of each user wanting to
run The Mops. For example, the user "jane" would need the
following commands run:

cp src/mopsrc *home*jane/.mopsrc

5. Create *usr*local/lib/mops and move the buttons and shaders:

mkdir *usr*local/lib/mops/

mv buttons/* *usr*local/lib/mops/

mv shader/*.sl* *usr*local/shaders/

If anything goes wrong, please consult the README and Setup.txt files
that accompany The Mops, or visit their website.

Log out from root. Log in as a regular user, and run The Mops as
follows:

*usr*local/mops/mops

You may wish to create a subdirectory within $HOME/mops called models
for saving 3D models.

3.6. Clean Up

Now that the installation is complete, you can remove from your system
all files that you no longer require (substituting version numbers
where required).

cd *usr*local/archives/

rm -rf BMRT2.6

rm -rf Mesa-3.4.1

Note: Be cautious when using rm -rf … make sure you are in the

correct directory, and the files and/or directories you wish to delete

are present.

4. Miscellaneous Information

Instead of a frequently asked questions section, here is information about some of the (almost embarassing) problems faced.

4.1. Lighting

The most frustrating problem, initially, was trying to figure out why everything was black — and then how to actually light objects up. In these "virtual worlds" where you are modelling objects, the worlds are created from scratch. There is no light in the world until you actually put a light source in it! The light sources then shine a given direction, illuminating things in their path (according to the surface properties of the objects). Make certain that your light source is:

1. pointing (rotated and translated) in the correct direction;

2. intense enough to actually cast discernable lighting.

4.2. Tutorials

The most basic thing a person would want to do with modelling/rendering packages is position a sphere on a surface, give it some lighting, and see the result. A decent tutorial should describe that first.

That said, The Mops has a wonderful first tutorial <http://www.informatik.uni-rostock.de/~rschultz/mops/tut1/tut1.html>.

5. Related Links

5.1. Graphics Libraries

Mesa <http://www.mesa3d.org/> - An OpenGL-compliant Graphics Library.

5.2. Graphics Renderers

BMRT <http://www.bmrt.org/> - The Blue Moon Rendering Toolkit.

POV-Ray <http://www.povray.org/> - The Persistence of Vision
Raytracer.

5.3. Graphics Modellers

The Mops <http://www.informatik.uni-rostock.de/~rschultz/mops/> - A 3D
modelling package that uses BMRT.

Blender <http://www.blender.nl> - Freeware modelling and rendering
suite of tools.

5.4. Miscellaneous Links

Here are some links that don't really fit into any other category, yet
are still worthwhile checking out if you are seriously considering
using your Linux computer as a 3D modelling and rendering machine.

3D Software for Linux <http://glide.xxedgexx.com/software.html> -
Contains most (if not all) links in this document and then some.

3D Modelling Software for Linux
<http://ntua.linuxberg.com/x11html/gra-3d.html> - Links to software
packages chiefly related to modelling.

3D Modelling and Rendering using Linux <http://linux3d.netpedia.net> -
A comprehensive site with articles and software that explains what
this document summarizes.

6. Acknowledgements

I would like to extend a heart-felt thanks to the developers of the software packages detailed in this document. The quality of their products is of a commercial level, yet they keep the spirit of free software alive. Well done!